# Series 117

This is a Ladybird Expert book, one of a series of titles for an adult readership. Written by some of the leading lights and outstanding communicators in their fields and published by one of the most trusted and well-loved names in books, the Ladybird Expert series provides clear, accessible and authoritative introductions, informed by expert opinion, to key subjects drawn from science, history and culture.

Endpaper map from *A School Map of English History* by Samuel Rawson Gardiner, 1914, courtesy of archive.org

Every effort has been made to ensure images are correctly attributed; however, if any omission or error has been made please notify the Publisher for correction in future editions.

MICHAEL JOSEPH

UK | USA | Canada | Ireland | Australia
India | New Zealand | South Africa

Michael Joseph is part of the Penguin Random House group of companies
whose addresses can be found at global.penguinrandomhouse.com

First published 2019
001

Printed in Italy by L.E.G.O. S.p.A.

A CIP catalogue record for this book is available from the British Library
ISBN: 978–0–718–18873–3

www.greenpenguin.co.uk

# The Battle of Trafalgar

**Sam Willis**

with illustrations by
Paul Young

Ladybird Books Ltd, London

On 26 May 1805 Napoleon crowned himself King of Italy in a lavish ceremony at the Duomo in Milan. The title 'King of Italy' had lain dormant for 249 years since the abdication of the Holy Roman Emperor Charles V in 1556, and now Napoleon, a Frenchman from modest roots on Corsica, had taken it for himself along with crucial territory in what is now northern Italy.

An extraordinary event in its own right, this was just the latest manifestation of Napoleon's takeover of Europe since the coup he had organized in Paris in 1799 which had transformed him from a general to First Consul of France and a dictator in everything but name. Soon after, the floodgates of his personal ambition truly opened. In 1802 this appointment, initially for a decade, became a 'life consulate' and changed in magnitude again in 1804 when he crowned himself Emperor of the French.

Threatened and appalled by Napoleon's apparently unstoppable and global ambition, Russia, Austria and Great Britain formed a coalition against him in 1803. The difficulty of containing the military and political genius of the leaders of Revolutionary and subsequently Napoleonic France is eloquently illustrated by its name, for this was the *Third* Coalition formed against France since the outbreak of the French Revolution: the first two had failed abysmally.

In September 1805, the Third Coalition made its first significant move by sending ships and troops to converge on Napoleon's new kingdom of Italy from north, south, east and west.

It was only at sea that the military power of France and her allies had been significantly checked.

At the first major naval battle of the Revolutionary Wars, known by the British as the Glorious First of June, of 1794, a French fleet was beaten by the British. In 1797, the two new allies of France – Spain and the Netherlands, now renamed the revolutionary-inspired 'Batavian Republic' – suffered twin defeats at the hands of the British: the Spanish at the Battle of St Vincent and the Dutch at the Battle of Camperdown. The following year Napoleon suffered the worst defeat of them all at the Battle of the Nile when his fleet, supporting the army he had landed for an invasion of Egypt, was annihilated by the British. In 1801, the fleet of Napoleon's newest allies, the Danes, was defeated at the Battle of Copenhagen.

Horatio Nelson, the son of a vicar from rural Norfolk but now a vice-admiral in the Royal Navy, distinguished himself at three of these battles and was personally responsible for the destruction of the French at the Nile. He was now showing the physical signs of life as a naval warrior.

In 1794, at an attack on a French town in Corsica, he was blinded in the right eye by shrapnel. Then in 1797, at the Battle of St Vincent, he was hit by flying debris so badly that when he coughed his intestines spilled out in a 'fist-sized hernia'. Nelson considered this wound 'trifling'. Five months later, at an invasion of the Spanish island of Santa Cruz de Tenerife in the Canary Islands, his arm was fractured by a musket ball and had to be amputated. A year after that, in August 1798, he was struck so hard in the head by a flying splinter at the Battle of the Nile that it exposed his skull and he believed he had been killed.

Fortunately for the British, he was wrong.

Napoleon was considering an invasion of England long before the outbreak of war with the Third Coalition, but from then on everything accelerated. The preparations were unprecedented. Two thousand invasion craft, including flat-bottomed boats each capable of transporting 55 infantry men, and larger sailing barges that could take up to 150 men each or guns, ammunition and horses, were built in ports all along northern France and the Low Countries. All were equipped with specially designed landing bridges. Harbours were dredged and basins dug to accommodate his flotilla.

Meanwhile, he gathered an army, unlike any seen before in France, at Boulogne, just thirty miles from the English coast. The soldiers were trained relentlessly in embarkation procedures, and at their height of skill the entire army, well over 170,000 men, could be embarked on the invasion craft in just ninety minutes. The soldiers were taught to use oars and naval artillery, even to swim in anticipation of the amphibious operation. They were given small-pox vaccinations, and the digging of wells was supervised by men responsible for the army's health. The men were skilled, lean, fit and disciplined, and to make sure that they retained their edge, Napoleon regularly inspected them. A triumphal column, based on Trajan's column in Rome, began to be erected in Boulogne in anticipation of a successful invasion.

Napoleon never actually launched this army against England but the column is still there, magnificent in its impotent pomp. Thwarted repeatedly by the Royal Navy, his own poor understanding of naval operations and the immense logistical and financial problems posed by such an operation, in late August 1805 he temporarily shelved his dream of conquering Britain and shifted his priorities to his new kingdom, Italy, now threatened from land and sea.

In late August 1805, Napoleon ordered his army at Boulogne to strike camp and march east, towards the Rhine. Soon afterwards he ordered his fleet at Cadiz, boosted by a fleet of his Spanish allies, to sail to the Mediterranean to provide naval support for the defence of Italy.

The Royal Navy had been waiting for just such an opportunity to engage the enemy. In the past ten months, a British fleet led by Nelson had sailed at least 10,000 miles in search of their enemy. They had begun their hunt in Sardinia, then sailed to Alexandria and back before heading to Toulon and back, via the Balearic Islands. From there they had sailed to Sicily before racing to Gibraltar and out of the Mediterranean. This first stage of hunting took five months. The subsequent four months took them across the Atlantic to Barbados, south to Trinidad, north to Antigua, back to Tetuán, opposite Gibraltar, and then north towards Spain, and then finally back to England. The enemy fleet slipped from their grasp time and again before taking refuge in Cadiz.

Nelson was now enjoying a rest at home, his first period ashore for twenty-seven months. His home was Merton Place in Surrey, near London, which he shared with his lover, Emma Hamilton, and his daughter, Horatia. It was the only house that this life-long sailor ever owned and lived in, and he adored it, a domestic fantasy come true.

It was here that, at dawn on 2 September, one of Nelson's close friends, Captain Henry Blackwood, arrived with news that the allied French and Spanish fleet, finally, had been found. Nelson was summoned to the Admiralty and ordered to resume his command off Cadiz.

By 1805, Nelson was already famous and the Royal Navy a cherished national institution that provided the British with wealth and security by defeating all-comers at sea.

As Nelson travelled to Portsmouth rumour flew ahead of him. By the time he arrived, thousands of well-wishers had gathered to cheer him on his way. He did his best to avoid them by taking a back-route to the sea but his groupies were too difficult to shake off and he was ambushed on the beach as he boarded the boat that would take him to his flagship, HMS *Victory*.

Three great cheers rose from the town walls. Ever alert to a crowd, Nelson swept off his hat in a heart-warming gesture of goodwill and gratitude, an open acknowledgement of thanks offered for glories bestowed and of good wishes sent for more glories desired.

The fleet Nelson joined off Cadiz was one of the most powerful war machines ever created. It consisted of 27 ships of the line manned by 17,000 sailors and marines. The largest vessels contained over 900 men. Each ship carried enough canvas to darken at least two acres of sky and those sails were supported and operated by 25 miles of rigging. Each ship contained at least 1,200 tons of food and the largest ships' magazines at least 45,000 pounds of gunpowder – the explosive capacity of 25 tons of TNT.

Seven were the mightiest of the warships, the First Rates. Two hundred feet long, armed with a hundred guns on three decks with masts well over 200 feet high, these monsters displaced as much as 3,500 tons of water. Twenty were two-decked ships ranging from 64 to 80 guns. These ships of the line were supported by four frigates – fast, single-decked warships – used to watch and shadow the enemy and to pass messages around the fleet.

The largest ships were made from the timber of as many as 5,000 substantial trees – around 300,000 cubic feet of timber. Those trees were a mixture of English oak, which provided the strength for the distinctive wine-glass-shaped skeleton of the ship, and beautifully straight Russian and Baltic pine, which was used for the masts and planks. Other sources of shipbuilding timber were India and America. These ships were not 'hearts of oak', therefore: it was perfectly possible in this period for a single ship to be built of timber from at least three different continents. They would take at least five years to build, some took twice as long.

It is almost impossible to overstate the size of such a fleet, but consider it this way: if it adopted the common cruising formation of a nautical mile between each ship, it would be thirty-two miles long.

The fleet Nelson joined represented a whole society at war. Sailors came from all over the British Isles, from America, Brazil, Canada, Denmark, Holland, Germany, Italy, Malta, Norway, Portugal, Sweden, Switzerland, India and the West Indies. One was Chinese. Some were even French and Spanish, now set on a trajectory to fight their countrymen.

Many were volunteers but many were also pressed, effectively kidnapped by a 'press gang' to serve in the Royal Navy.

Not all were men. Numerous women sailed with these ships, some in an official capacity as officers' wives, some unofficially, some even in disguise.

Not all were adults. Children served on these ships as well, with as many as thirty on the largest vessels. The youngest boy on board HMS *Victory* was twelve.

The few cabins were all reserved for the senior officers. Ordinary sailors had just fourteen inches – about the width of a standard computer keyboard – in which to sling their hammock. Perhaps even worse was the lack of toilet facilities for the lower ranks in need of more than a 'piss dale' – a type of lead guttering that took urine overboard. For the 810 people on board who were not petty officers or above, there were six round holes in planks at the bow, all next to each other and all exposed to the weather.

The French and Spanish fleets were different from the British and also from each other.

French warships tended to be swifter and lighter than either their Spanish or British counterparts, built for trade protection rather than for blockade, fleet battle or pure prestige. Nonetheless they were greatly admired, and Nelson sailed into battle at Trafalgar with seven ships that had either been captured from the French or whose design had directly inspired a British version.

The Spanish ships were unusually magnificent. Unlike the British or French they were typically made of tropical hardwoods such as teak or mahogany which were almost impervious to rot and so dense as to be like natural armour.

The finest of them all was the *Santísima Trinidad*, the largest warship in the world, the only four-decker, and the only ship to mount 130 guns. She displaced nearly 5,000 tons.

Both French and Spanish navies, however, were struggling with manpower because neither had the sophisticated administrative and logistical infrastructure of the British, which had allowed the Royal Navy to keep its ships well manned with skilled sailors, and those men healthy over a long period.

The unfortunate man in charge of this unfortunate fleet was the multi-barrelled Vice-Admiral Pierre-Charles-Jean-Baptiste-Silvestre de Villeneuve. A man of immense naval experience, Villeneuve had foundered in the service of his exacting Emperor.

In the preceding two years, Napoleon had concocted seven separate invasion plans for the British Isles, none of which had been grounded in the complex practical realities of naval warfare. He had then blamed Villeneuve for his own faults.

'*Villeneuve is a miserable individual*', he wrote, '*who must be shamefully thrown out. He has no strategy, no courage, no general interest, and would sacrifice everything to save his own skin.*'

A replacement was dispatched from Paris, but Villeneuve heard of his imminent arrival and, encouraged by rumours that the British blockading squadron had been temporarily reduced, decided to act, to try to take his fleet to defend Napoleon's Italy as he had been ordered.

Thousands lined the walls and rooftops of Cadiz to watch this fleet leave, in absolute silence. There had not been a significant Spanish or French naval victory over the British for almost a quarter of a century. There had been nothing but defeats.

As soon as Nelson heard that the Allied fleet was at sea, he worried that it would return to Cadiz. He wanted, and the country needed, a battle of total annihilation, but such a battle could only realistically be achieved if the enemy either chose to stand and fight or was forced to do so. The first was extremely unlikely to happen and the second extremely difficult to achieve.

His idea was to divide his fleet into two columns and cut the enemy line in two locations, towards the centre and towards the rear, thus severing the van (the 'head' of the enemy fleet) from its body. In the chaotic action that would inevitably ensue Nelson believed that his healthier, better-trained sailors with their better guns would triumph over the enemy. A key factor in his thinking was that the British had guns called carronades, which their enemy did not. These were large-calibre short-range weapons, and they were extremely destructive.

He also knew that his tactics were dangerous. There were few or no guns in the bows of a sailing warship, and so the approach to the enemy at right angles to their line would be exceptionally risky: while the enemy would be able to fire the full force of their broadsides, his ships would be unable to offer anything in return.

To mitigate that risk, he would attack under full sail and place his most powerful ships at the head of each column. He had faith that his new tactics would, in his own words, 'surprise and confound' the enemy.

Longitud del Meridiano de Cadiz

Longitud Occidental del Meridiano de Cartagena

Nelson knew that in the chaos of a naval battle nothing was certain and so he issued a simple order:

'*No captain can do very wrong if he places his ship alongside that of an enemy.*'

It seems like an obvious thing to say, but consider the men who were serving under him. This was no 'Band of Brothers', the description he gave his captains at the Battle of the Nile. They sailed in the same navy and they shared enemies but the fleet had been scratched together from a variety of different squadrons. Only eleven of his twenty-seven captains had ever sailed with him before and only six had ever commanded a ship in a fleet battle before. From the moment he arrived off Cadiz until the day of the fight, Nelson had just three weeks to get to know his captains, share with them his ideas and lay out his expectations of their behaviour.

A man who was always acutely aware of his own ability and who was more than happy to tell everyone about it, he certainly enjoyed the effect that his ideas had on his new commanders. He described the moment to Emma: '*when I came to explain the Nelson touch, some shed tears, all approved, as it was new, it was singular, it was simple.*'

It was certainly a unique approach to naval leadership at the time, a contrast not only to the French and Spanish but to the other commanders in the Royal Navy. All were bound up in a rigid system of signals and instructions and less willing to take the risks necessary to secure absolute victory over a prepared, powerful and larger enemy fleet.

With the French and Spanish fleet now at sea and visible, Nelson divided his fleet into two columns and set all sail. He led one column in the *Victory* and his friend Cuthbert Collingwood, who had joined the navy at the age of eleven and was now a fifty-seven-year-old vice-admiral, led the other in the *Royal Sovereign*.

As they approached the enemy, Nelson's friend Henry Blackwood questioned the wisdom of Nelson leading his line into battle. This was contrary to his original sailing instructions, in which HMS *Temeraire* had been listed at the head of the line. This was the ship that J. M. W. Turner would later immortalize in his painting *The Fighting Temeraire*.

Nelson agreed with Blackwood and ordered Captain Harvey of the *Temeraire* to take her allotted position at the head of the line but, just as she started to surge past the *Victory*, Nelson changed his mind, incapable of letting someone else lead his fleet into battle.

It was one of several moments of the battle that caught the public imagination in its aftermath and was later immortalized by the poet Henry Newbolt:

> 'The *Victory* led
> To her flag it was due
> Tho' the *Temeraires* thought themselves admirals too
> But Lord Nelson he hailed them
> With masterful grace
> Cap'n Harvey, I'll thank you to keep in your place.'

The fleets closed, but in the light winds it was at an excruciatingly slow pace, no more than 1.5 knots, that is 1.5 miles per hour, or a third of a standard adult's walking pace. The ordeal of endurance and terror that lay ahead was thus made unimaginably worse by its prolonged anticipation.

The size of the enemy fleet would have become increasingly apparent. At first it appeared 'like a wood' on the horizon but ever so slowly the ships would have emerged as individual vessels, and the British sailors would have been able to count thirty-three ships of the line – that is six more than their own fleet – and seven frigates and smaller vessels. They would also have noted from the distinctive shapes on the horizon that the fleet included four First Rate ships, each of them larger than the three British First Rates, and one of them, the *Santísima Trinidad*, the largest warship in the world. The British were outnumbered and they knew it.

In these last tense moments, Nelson decided to 'amuse' the fleet and hoisted a signal:

*England expects that every man will do his duty.*

This was the first significant use of a new signalling code, which had only just been given to the fleet. Before this an admiral had only been able to send a very restricted number of signals relating to pre-prescribed manoeuvres or instructions. The new code, however, allowed for far more flexibility – essentially it allowed an admiral to 'chat' to his men.

It is so indicative of Nelson's emotional intelligence that he immediately grasped the potential of this new system. Although the signal may appear to us bland, it received the most enormous cheer throughout the fleet.

'The shout it aroused', said Blackwood, was 'truly sublime'.

It is also possible to read in this signal a level of uncertainty. Why would Nelson need to remind his captains of their duty – of what was expected of them?

The answer is that Nelson knew his history, and he knew that, in spite of the overwhelming story of British naval success in the recent years, there had also been examples of incompetence, confusion, outright cowardice and mutiny that had marred the conduct of the Royal Navy.

Nelson flew that signal, therefore, not just to 'amuse' the fleet, but because he needed to remind his men of their duty as they sailed towards injury and death.

The coming battle would test his men as they had never been tested before. The total firepower of both armies at Waterloo amounted to just 7.3 per cent of the firepower that was about to be unleashed at Trafalgar.

The men lay down next to their guns. British gunnery doctrine rested entirely on proximity to their enemy and sustained ferocity of fire. They would, therefore, have to withstand the full force of the enemy before they could fire back. Lying down, making their bodies as small a target as possible to a gun trained horizontally, increased their chance of survival until that moment.

On the *Victory* alone thirty men died and twenty were wounded before they fired a single shot at their enemy.

Collingwood's column was the first into action but he had not acted quite as Nelson had expected. Seeing one of the Spanish commanders, Vice-Admiral Don Ignacio María de Álava, raise his flag further up the line from where Nelson wanted him to break it, Collingwood had been lured as a mackerel to a feather and he cut the enemy line sixteen ships from the end, rather than eleven.

To make matters worse, the other ships in his squadron struggled to sail at a similar speed to the *Royal Sovereign* and did not all come into action together. Only eight of his eleven made it into action in the first group.

Collingwood, therefore, noble as he may have been, was now massively outnumbered.

Forty-five minutes later, Nelson broke the enemy line astern of the French flagship, the *Bucentaur*, and unleashed a broadside and a 68-pound carronade loaded with a roundshot and 500 musket balls through the stern windows of the French ship.

The *Victory*, however, did not break through the enemy line as intended because the French had accidentally staggered their line. This meant that once past the *Bucentaur*, there were more ships to contend with. One of them was the *Redoutable*, a large 74-gun ship commanded by one of the best officers in the French navy, Captain Jean Lucas, who immediately brought his smaller ship alongside the *Victory*.

The initial exchanges are barely imaginable. Hundreds of men died in the first broadsides alone as the largest of the British ships smashed through the enemy line. Holes were punched through hulls, splinters flew in clouds, sails tore, yards – and even masts – snapped and collapsed. The largest masts on a First Rate man of war were so big that they were made up of as many as six separate pieces of timber; they had a diameter of almost a metre and a circumference of over three metres. When the lowest masts collapsed everything above them came down – tons and tons of timber, wooden blocks, iron stanchions, rope, canvas and men – like a house falling out of the sky and crushing anything it landed on.

On the poop deck of HMS *Victory* eight marines were killed by a single double-headed shot and on the *Revenge* a child was brutally cut down. 'He was a youth of not more than twelve or thirteen years of age . . . killed on the quarter-deck by grape-shot, his body greatly mutilated, his entrails being driven and scattered against the larboard side.'

In amongst this carnage, women tended the injured, and boys, known as powder monkeys, carried gunpowder in tubular wooden or canvas cases, similar in size to a modern fire extinguisher, between the ship's magazine and their gun crew. This was the only way that the flow of powder could be controlled in a relatively safe way. At this crucial stage in the battle the safety of each ship and its efficiency as a fighting unit rested on a human chain of children.

The wounded were carried down to the lowest deck of the ship, below the waterline where there was no ventilation but where it was relatively safe from enemy fire. On HMS *Victory* one of the wounded being carried down the companionway ladders, among a group of forty bleeding men, had a handkerchief over his face.

It was Nelson. To avoid dispiriting his men he had asked for his face to be covered.

He was still lucid but he had been shot from a marksman in the rigging of Lucas's *Redoutable*, and the wound was a bad one. The musket ball had entered, and broken, his left shoulder, broken some ribs, burst a lung, broken his back and severed his bronchial artery. He felt the ball break his spine and now felt arterial blood pulsing into his lungs. He knew he was a dead man.

We do not know for certain if the shot was deliberate or simply lucky, but a modern reconstruction of the angles involved, using identical weaponry and a life-size target, suggests that the shot was both possible and repeatable, even given the chaos of battle. It is quite possible that the marksman had marked him out in his distinctive uniform with his imitation medals on the breast.

Nelson was taken to the *Victory*'s surgeon, William Beatty, who quickly realized that the wound was fatal. He was given water and lemonade and company: he was not left alone. Beatty, busy with other casualties, came and went, checking on his condition. Thomas Hardy, *Victory*'s captain, also came and went but he had a special relationship with Nelson and a special role to play. In one of his final moments of lucidity Nelson, longing for human contact, said, 'Kiss me Hardy,' and Hardy did.

Nelson survived for three hours in the dark lantern-lit cockpit, surrounded by the screams of men being operated on, buckets of amputated limbs, streams of blood on the deck and with the incessant thundering of cannon and shouting of men.

Before he died he was told that fourteen of the enemy ships had surrendered. 'That is well,' he replied, 'but I had bargained for twenty.' His lengthening periods of silence gave way to outbursts of anxiety – about Emma, about Horatia, about his fleet – but finally he became silent, the storm in his body passed, and his soul drifted away.

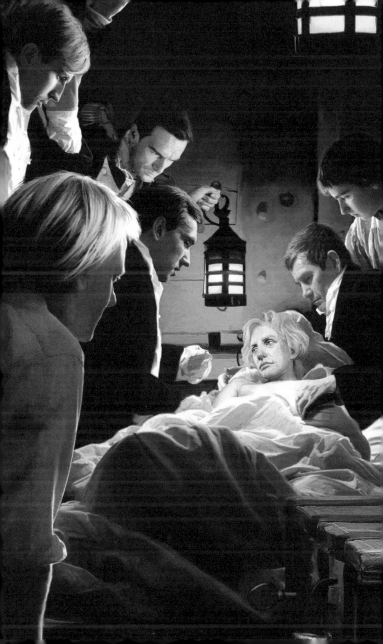

The battle, of course, continued without Nelson, who was shot at 13.15, just fifty minutes after the first exchange of shots. It continued with intense ferocity until 17.50 – that is for another four hours and thirty-five minutes.

The battle, which had begun in isolated pockets around the *Victory* and the *Royal Sovereign*, spread up and down the curved Allied line as more and more British ships came into action. The decapitated head of the enemy fleet, meanwhile, turned to assist its stricken body. This squadron, commanded by Rear Admiral Pierre Dumanoir le Pelley, failed to impact the battle as it might have done: he reacted late to Villeneuve's orders to turn and sail back to the fight, and when he did so only four ships actually made the manoeuvre and then baulked at the challenge posed by the British and fled.

Several British ships also failed to engage as was expected, some for want of courage or understanding of the plan; others for reasons of physical disability. Nonetheless, for those ships that were engaged, the battle became a competition of gunnery and seamanship skill, of physical endurance and mental strength, and that competition was won unequivocally by the British. The heaviest casualty rate for the British fleet was suffered by the 74-gun *Colossus*, which suffered 200 dead or wounded, but she inflicted two and a half times her own losses on the enemy.

The equation was simple: the British killed more men, more quickly and in more ships, than the French or Spanish. Gradually the Allied flagships surrendered to prevent further unnecessary bloodshed, and the end of the battle, more than five hours after it had started, was marked by the titanic explosion of the French ship *Achille*.

By no means was the battle the end of that dreadful day, however. Ever since the Allies had opened fire around midday, a horrible, lumpy swell had thrown the ships this way and that, and such heavy swells were always signs of an approaching storm.

It hit as daylight faded. Many described it as a hurricane. It was certainly a storm of such ferocity that few of these life-long sailors had ever seen its like or would ever see it again. Something of great significance was revealed by this storm, most eloquently summed up by Villeneuve's astonished Chief of Staff.

*'It came on to blow a gale of wind, and the English immediately set to work to shorten sail and reef the topsails, with as much regularity and order as if their ships had not been fighting a dreadful battle. We were all amazement, wondering what the English seamen could be made of. All our seamen were either drunk or disabled . . .'*

In such extremes was the real difference between the Allies and the British laid bare, the measure of competence upon which Nelson had built his entire battle plan.

Throughout all of this, Collingwood unexpectedly found himself in charge. An altogether different leader to Nelson, Collingwood nonetheless had unique talents of his own. He was, in particular, a measured and a talented diplomat. In the battle's aftermath he went on to make a number of extremely wise and far-reaching command decisions, most notably allowing all of the captured Spanish prisoners to return freely to Spain. This was instrumental in building a bridge between Britain and Spain which eventually led to the Spanish changing sides in 1808 and helping the British tighten the noose around Napoleon's neck.

Of the thirty-three Allied line-of-battle ships that began the fight, seventeen were captured and one destroyed, nearly double Nelson's astonishing haul at the Battle of the Nile in 1798. Trafalgar created an entirely new perception of victory; it was the annihilation of the enemy fleet that Britain had desperately needed and Nelson had dreamt of.

Of the eighteen ships wrenched from the enemy, only four prizes were eventually taken into the Royal Navy. The rest of them were either wrecked in the storm or destroyed, an exceptionally high attrition rate for these behemoth wooden battleships that, given their construction techniques and the limitations of weaponry, were incredibly difficult to destroy.

We still don't know how many in the Allied fleet were casualties. A rough estimate is that 4,400 died and perhaps 2,500 were wounded. In comparison, 449 British sailors died and 1,242 were wounded, far higher figures than in any other naval battle of the Revolutionary or Napoleonic wars. Of the thirty British flag officers and captains present, a third were either killed or wounded.

The Frenchmen who were not killed on those eighteen ships were all taken prisoner. Barely a third of the French sailors who left Cadiz ever made it home.

The fate of the three navies' commanders is indicative of so much of the story of Trafalgar: of British seapower gloriously worshipped; of Spanish courage generously respected; of French honour shockingly mistreated.

Nelson was the embodiment of seapower, and seapower was revered by the British. His body, preserved in brandy, camphor and myrrh, was carefully brought home. His funeral, coffin and tomb were fit for a king.

Admiral Don Federico Gravina, the Spanish fleet commander, died in Cadiz from wounds received in the battle. He had fought with immense courage against three enemy ships and had safely withdrawn his forces to Cadiz through the storm. The Spanish public could read between the lines of the defeat and they adored him. He was buried amid splendid pomp in the magnificent Panteón de Marinos Ilustres in Cadiz.

Villeneuve spent a short time in England until released on parole in late 1805. This experienced and honourable man immediately returned to France and tried to re-enter military service but with no success. And then, on 22 April 1806, he was found dead in a hotel room with six stab wounds in the left lung and one in the heart. To the surprise of many, who failed to believe so many wounds could be self-inflicted, a verdict of suicide was recorded. Whispers suggested he had been killed on the orders of Napoleon.

Napoleon raged at his navy's performance at Trafalgar. He saw treachery where there was none and spat in the faces of those who had risked their lives.

To increase his distaste for all things naval, a matter of weeks after Trafalgar, Napoleon's beloved army won the greatest of all of his many and great military victories at the Battle of Austerlitz.

His Grand Armée which had struck camp at Boulogne reached the Danube, 600 kilometres away, in just four weeks. It was the first time in the history of warfare that so many men had moved so far so fast. No one expected their arrival and the result was that Napoleon captured an entire Austrian army led by the Holy Roman Emperor Francis II and the Tsar of Russia, Alexander I. He also captured Vienna, the first time the city had fallen in its history. As a direct result the Holy Roman Empire, which had been founded by Charlemagne in AD 962, ceased to exist.

In the aftermath of Trafalgar, therefore, the situation in central Europe was as dire as it could possibly be. At sea problems also continued. In spite of the massive victory, the Royal Navy did not suddenly and magically 'control the seas'. There was an entire French fleet in Brest which had played no part at all in the Trafalgar campaign, a smaller force in Rochefort and a combined force of French and Spanish ships still in Cadiz. None of the French or Spanish ships in the Mediterranean were affected by Trafalgar nor were those that patrolled the sea routes in the East Indies. Napoleon, meanwhile, threw money into rebuilding his fleet.

The Royal Navy's day job, protecting the trade of Britain and her allies, moving and supplying the troops still fighting Napoleon on Continental Europe, finding the enemy ships and blockading them in their ports, continued.

Trafalgar, therefore, did not bring a sudden end to the Napoleonic wars, which continued for another decade, but Napoleon never recovered from the loss of his ships and he never directly challenged the British at sea again. His new ships were poorly built and weak, and the Spanish navy simply never recovered: Spain did not launch another naval warship until 1853.

After Trafalgar, British naval superiority was never absolute but it was enough to stop Napoleon from launching ambitious trans-oceanic campaigns. British seapower was also sufficient to guarantee Britain's economic prosperity by defending and expanding her maritime empire. This in turn helped Britain pay for more ships and subsidize her allies in the Continental war against Napoleon, who remained trapped in a whirlpool of war that swallowed all of his resources and ultimately led to his defeat in 1814.

For the scale of victory, and for the death of the most brilliant naval commander who has ever lived, Trafalgar became the most famous naval battle in history but it also became one of Britain's greatest collective sorrows. Nelson's death is perhaps only comparable as an outpouring of national grief to the death of Diana, Princess of Wales, in 1997. Nelson's funeral lasted for five days and, as he requested, his coffin was made from the mast of the French flagship *L'Orient* at the Battle of the Nile in 1798. He was buried in St Paul's Cathedral in a tomb which is significantly more ornate than many British monarchs'. Interest in Nelson never waned and in 1835 a newly cleared area in London between St Paul's and Parliament was named Trafalgar Square. In 1843 Nelson's Column was commissioned and the diminutive ghost of Nelson has watched over Britain ever since.

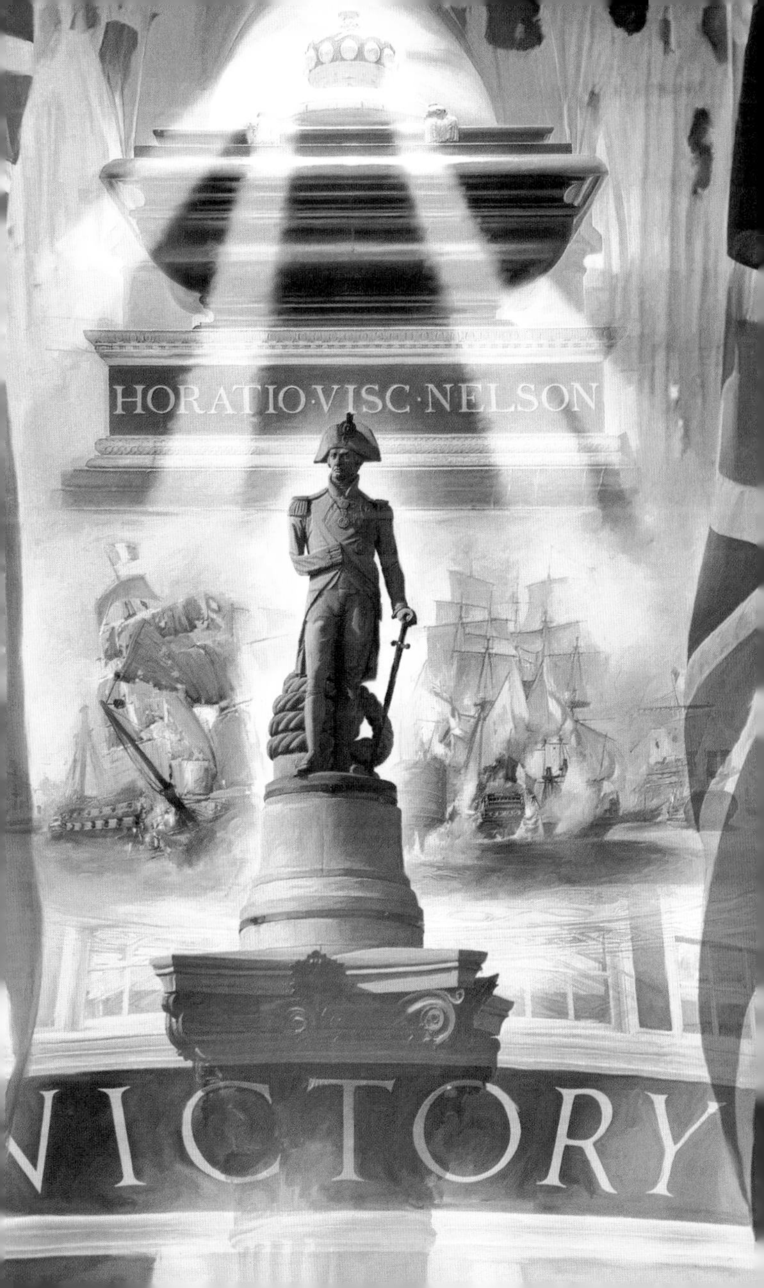
HORATIO·VISC·NELSON
VICTORY

## Further Reading

Nicholas Blake *Steering to Glory: A Day in the Life of a Line of Battle Ship*

Sam Willis *The Fighting Temeraire*

Sam Willis *In the Hour of Victory: the Royal Navy at War in the Age of Nelson*

Roger Knight *The Pursuit of Victory: the Life and Achievement of Horatio Nelson*